Table of Contents

...	1
Introduction	4
Spicy Dame Cocktail	5
Chicken Curry Soup	7
Smoky Lentil Chili	9
Spicy Bloody Maria	12
Bacon and Potato Soup	14
Spicy Margarita	16
Dirty Dr. Pepper Cocktail	18
Ham and Pea Soup	20
Cream of Celery Soup	22
Crunchy Rhubarb	24
Minestrone Soup	26
Hot Chocolate	29
Crimson Spice	31
Pumpkin Soup	33
Spicy Tomato Juice	35
Spicy Watermelon Cocktail	37
Michelada	39
Thai Style Potato Soup	41
Barley Cream Soup	44
Jalapeño syrup	46
French Cider and Potato Soup	48
Cauliflower Soup	50
Spicy Green Juice	53
Lemon Delicious Pudding	55
Butterscotch pudding	57
Jalapeño Margaritas	59
Winter Warmer Soup	61
Leek and Potato Soup	64
Thai Coconut Fish Stew	66
Spicy Tequila Sunrise	68
Conclusion	70

Spicy Recipes for the Winter Holidays
"Spicy Recipes to Combat Winter Chills!"

BY: Ida Smith

Copyright © 2020 by Ida Smith. All Rights Reserved.

License Notes

This book is licensed for your personal enjoyment only. This book may not be re-sold or given away to other people. If you would like to share this book with another person, please purchase an additional copy for each recipient. If you're reading this book and did not purchase it, or it was not purchased for your use only, then please return to your favorite ebook retailer and purchase your own copy. Thank you for respecting the hard work of this author.

Introduction

Winter meals hit differently when they are spicy and warm, and this is why this Cookbook focuses on 30 spicy recipes that will help you enjoy the best of your winter holidays!!

Spicy Dame Cocktail

When we talk of spicy winter cocktails that exude class and style, this cocktail takes a good lead.

Preparation Time: 04 Minutes
Cooking time: Nil
Yield: 1

Ingredient List:

- 3 oz ginger syrup
- 2 oz vodka
- 1 sliced cucumber
- 1 sliced jalapeño
- 3 mint leaves.

Preparation:
1. Drop the ingredients in a shaker.
2. Shake well.
3. Strain into a glass of ice. Garnish with cucumber and jalapeño slices.

Chicken Curry Soup

Simply delicious!!
   Preparation Time: 10 Minutes
   Cooking time: 20 Minutes
   Yield: 2

Ingredient List:

- 1 diced carrot
- 1 minced garlic clove
- 1 tablespoon curry paste (green)
- 1 tablespoon canola oil
- 2 handfuls green onions (chopped)
- 2 boneless chicken breasts (skinless and cubed)
- 8 oz coconut milk
- 2 tablespoons lemon juice
- 1 cup chicken broth

Preparation:
1. Sauté the carrot and garlic in a wok of oil.
2. Cook for 3 minutes.
3. Add in the paste and milk.
4. Cook for 3 minutes.
5. Add the chicken and broth.
6. Throw in the onions and lemon juice.
7. Cook for 4 minutes.
8. Serve.

Smoky Lentil Chili

A pot of delicious and spicy awesomeness!
> **Preparation Time:** 07 Minutes
> **Cooking time:** 23 Minutes
> **Yield:** 4

Ingredient List:

- 1 lb ground beef
- 1 teaspoon ground cumin
- 1 chopped red onion
- 2 tablespoons chili powder
- 1 diced red pepper
- 1 minced garlic clove
- 1 tablespoon oil
- 1 diced medium-sized carrot
- 1 diced green pepper
- 1 tablespoon adobe sauce
- 1 teaspoon salt
- 1 pinch dried oregano
- 2 cups water
- 1 tablespoon tomato paste
- 15 oz roasted diced tomatoes
- 2 cups rinsed beans (kidney and black)
- 1 tablespoon smoked Paprika
- 1 cup rinsed lentils
- 4 tablespoons lemon juice
- 1 pinch ground cinnamon
- 7 oz corn kernels

Preparation:
1. Sauté garlic and onions in a pot of oil.
2. Cook for 2 minutes.
3. Throw in the beef. Cook for 4 minutes.
4. Add the carrots, chili, Paprika, peppers, sauce, salt, cinnamon, oregano, cumin, and tomato paste. Cook-stir for 3 minutes.
5. Add the lemon juice, tomatoes, and water.
6. Cook for 6 minutes.
7. Add the beans, corn, and lentils.
8. Cook for 12 minutes.
9. Serve.

Spicy Bloody Maria

A glass of Bloody Maria with a garnish of spice!!
Preparation Time: 04 Minutes
Cooking time: Nil
Yield: 1

Ingredient List:

- 1 tablespoon horseradish
- 2 dashes Worcestershire sauce
- 2 dashes Tabasco sauce
- 2 oz tequila
- 2 dashes pepper
- 2 tablespoons lemon juice
- 1 tablespoon celery salt

Preparation:
1. Put the ingredients in a glass one after the other.
2. Stir well.
3. Garnish with celery and lemon wedge.

Bacon and Potato Soup

It is easy to prepare this delicious spicy soup!!

Preparation Time: 04 Minutes
Cooking time: 12 Minutes
Yield: 3
Ingredient List:

- 1 teaspoon Worcestershire sauce
- 2 tablespoons hot sauce
- 2 handfuls chopped cooked bacon
- 8 tablespoons Parmesan cheese

- 2 cups milk
- 15 oz chopped hash brown potatoes
- 1 cup fried onions
- 5 oz cream of celery soup
- 1 chopped jalapeño

Preparation:
1. Put the bacon, sauces, cheese, soup, jalapeño, potatoes, and milk in a pot. Cook-stir for 10 minutes.
2. Serve and garnish with onions.
3. Enjoy.

Spicy Margarita

Let's commence this recipe book with a glass of spicy margarita!! Shall we?
Preparation Time: 04 Minutes
Cooking time: Nil
Yield: 1

Ingredient List:

- 1 oz orange liqueur
- 2 tablespoons lemon juice
- 3 oz tequila
- 1 oz agave syrup
- 1 pinch salt
- 3 jalapeño slices (deseeded)
- 1 lemon slice

Preparation:
1. Dab the rim of the glass with salt. Set aside
2. Drop all the ingredients in a shaker of ice.
3. Shake well.
4. Strain into your glass.
5. Garnish with a slice of deseeded jalapeño.
6. Enjoy.

Dirty Dr. Pepper Cocktail

Not your regular Dr. Pepper!!
Preparation Time: 03 Minutes
Cooking time: Nil
Yield: 1

Ingredient List:

- 1 can Coca Cola
- 2 oz cinnamon alcohol
- 2 oz Amaretto

Preparation:
1. Combine all three ingredients in your glass of ice.
2. Stir.
3. Enjoy.

Ham and Pea Soup

Do you have leftover ham in the refrigerator and wonder what to do with it?

Just combine it with pea and some ingredients, and you'd have one of the spiciest and most delicious winter soups ever!!

Preparation Time: 05 Minutes
Cooking time: 50 Minutes
Yield: 2
Ingredient List:

- 1 tablespoon salt
- 1 tablespoon pepper
- 3 tablespoons ground jalapeño

- 250g split peas
- 2 cups water
- 1 minced garlic clove
- 1 tablespoon oil
- 1 chopped onion
- 300g ham

Preparation:
1. Sauté the garlic and onion in a pan of oil.
2. Cook for 2 minutes.
3. Throw in the ham and peas.
4. Add water, jalapeño, pepper, and salt.
5. Cook till the peas pop.
6. Serve.

Cream of Celery Soup

No store-bought versions can compare to this homemade version!!!
Preparation Time: 10 Minutes
Cooking time: 15 Minutes
Yield: 2

Ingredient List:

- 1 minced garlic clove
- 1 tablespoon canola oil
- 3 tablespoons flour
- 1 cup chopped celery
- 1 cup broth
- 1 chopped yellow onion
- 1 pinch sugar
- 2 tablespoons ground jalapeño
- 1 cup milk
- 1 pinch salt
- 1 pinch ground pepper

Preparation:
1. Sauté the garlic, celery, and onion in a wok of oil.
2. Cook for 4 minutes.
3. Throw in the flour.
4. Cook for 45 seconds.
5. Add in the broth, sugar, salt, pepper, jalapeño, and milk. Cook-stir for 4 minutes.
6. Serve

Crunchy Rhubarb

It's crunchy, spicy and creamy!!
   Preparation Time: 10 Minutes
   Cooking time: 20 Minutes
   Yield: 3

Ingredient List:

- 50g melted butter
- 2 tablespoons grated coconut
- 2 cups cooked rhubarb
- 4 tablespoons flour
- 4 tablespoons sugar
- 1 pinch ground cinnamon
- 4 tablespoons rolled oats
- 1 tablespoon brown sugar
- 1 cup milk
- 1 tablespoon custard powder
- 3 tablespoons almonds (flaked)

Preparation:
1. Preheat the oven to 358 degrees F.
2. Mix the custard powder, sugar, and milk in a pan. Heat for 3 minutes.
3. Pour the rhubarb at the base of a baking pan.
4. Spread the milk custard over the rhubarb.
5. Mix the butter, flour, brown sugar, oats, coconut, and cinnamon in a bowl.
6. Add the mixture over the custard.
7. Bake till the mixture is crunchy and brown.
8. Serve and enjoy.

Minestrone Soup

We have never tasted a soup exotic and spicy like this!!
Preparation Time: 10 Minutes
Cooking time: 20 Minutes
Yield: 3

Ingredient List:

- 1 diced celery stalk
- 1 diced medium onion
- 1 tablespoon olive oil
- 1 diced carrot
- 2 minced garlic cloves
- 1 handful dried basil
- 1 pinch dried oregano
- 1 cup chopped green beans
- 1 tablespoon pepper
- 1 tablespoon salt
- 7 oz crushed tomatoes
- 14 oz diced tomatoes
- 1 jalapeño crushed
- 7 oz kidney beans
- 3 cups broth
- 1 pack pasta
- 1 handful chopped basil
- 3 tablespoons grated cheese

Preparation:
1. Sauté the garlic, carrot, onion, jalapeño, and celery in a pan of oil.
2. Cook for 4 minutes.
3. Add in the oregano, green beans, pepper, salt, and basil.
4. Cook for 3 minutes.
5. Add the tomatoes and broth.
6. Cook for 6 minutes.
7. Add the pasta and kidney beans.
8. Serve and garnish with basil and cheese.

Hot Chocolate

This cup of delicious chocolatey awesomeness will keep you warm on lonely winter nights!
Preparation Time: 04 Minutes
Cooking time: 08 Minutes
Yield: 3

Ingredient List:

- 3 tablespoons cocoa powder
- 1 cup chocolate chips (dark)
- 2 cups milk
- 1 tablespoon pepper

Preparation:
1. Combine the chips, pepper, cocoa powder, and milk in a pan.
2. Stir overheat till it's melted.
3. Serve.
4. Enjoy.

Crimson Spice

Incredible!!!

Preparation Time: 08 Minutes
Cooking time: 50 Minutes
Yield: 1
Ingredient List:

- 1 star anise
- 1 cinnamon stick
- 1 sliced ginger piece

- 1 quart cranberry juice cocktail
- 4 cups chilled Champagne
- 4 tablespoons brandy
- 20 cranberries

Preparation:
1. Put the juice, cinnamon, ginger, and star anise in a pot.
2. Cook for 50 minutes.
3. Allow chilling and strain into a pitcher.
4. Chill before serving.

Pumpkin Soup

Who needs a winter soup for dunking??
   Preparation Time: 05 Minutes
   Cooking time: 10 Minutes
   Yield: 3

Ingredient List:

- 1 handful sliced onions (different colors)
- 1kg chopped pumpkin (peeled and seeded)
- 1 tablespoon salt
- 1 tablespoon pepper
- 100ml water
- 300ml chicken broth
- 1 minced garlic clove
- 2 jalapeño peppers
- 1 cup cream

Preparation:
1. Put the onion, pumpkin, jalapeño, water, and broth in a pot.
2. Boil for 8 minutes.
3. Set aside to cool.
4. Transfer to a blender.
5. Blend for 3 minutes.
6. Season with pepper and salt.
7. Add in cream.
8. Serve.

Spicy Tomato Juice

When do they ask what else a tomato can do? Give them a taste of this juice!!
Preparation Time: 04 Minutes
Cooking time: Nil
Yield: 2

Ingredient List:

- 1 minced jalapeño
- 5 celery stalks
- 1 pinch celery seed
- 1 pinch coarse salt
- 1 sliced red chili
- 1 pinch pepper
- 2 tablespoons lemon juice
- 5 handfuls chopped tomatoes

Preparation:
1. Drop the ingredients except for the sliced red chili in a food processor.
2. Blend well.
3. Serve and garnish with the red chili.

Spicy Watermelon Cocktail

We were not sure how it would come out at first, but then we tried, and voila!!!
We have the best spicy watermelon cocktail recipe right here!
Preparation Time: 03 Minutes
Cooking time: Nil
Yield: 1

Ingredient List:

- 2 oz watermelon juice
- 1 oz jalapeno syrup
- 1 sprig mint
- 2 oz white tequila
- 1 chilled watermelon slice
- 1 oz lemon juice
- 1 tablespoon horseradish
- 1 lemon slice
- 1 tablespoon sugar

Preparation:
1. Chill the glass first.
2. Coat the rim of the glass with sugar
3. Pour watermelon juice, tequila, ice, lemon juice, syrup, and horseradish in a shaker.
4. Shake well.
5. Strain into glass
6. Rub the lemon wedges around the glass rim.
7. Garnish with watermelon slice and mint.
8. Enjoy.

Michelada

From Mexico with a lot of love!!!!
   Preparation Time: 04 Minutes
   Cooking time: Nil
   Yield: 1

Ingredient List:

- 2 tablespoons tomato juice
- 1 can lager beer
- 2 splashes hot sauce
- 1 tablespoon soy sauce
- 1 tablespoon Worcestershire sauce
- 1 tablespoon Tajin
- 1 tablespoon lemon juice
- 1 lemon slice

Preparation:
1. Scoop tajin with the lemon slice and rub across the rim of the glass.
2. Drop the ingredients in the glass.
3. Add ice. Garnish with a lemon slice.

Thai Style Potato Soup

Winter in Thai style!!!

Preparation Time: 10 Minutes
Cooking time: 1 Hour 20 Minutes
Yield: 8
Ingredient List:

- 4 chopped large-sized onions
- 6 tablespoons minced ginger
- 500ml coconut milk

- 8 tablespoons sesame oil
- 4 cups chopped mixed herbs
- 4 tablespoons lemon juice
- 4 tablespoons Thai curry paste (red)
- 4 liters chicken broth
- 6 tablespoons chopped chilies
- 4 tablespoons sugar (brown)
- 4 peeled large-sized sweet potatoes (chunked)

Preparation:
1. Preheat your oven to 404 degrees F.
2. Put the onion, 250ml of oil, sugar, chilies, and potatoes in a baking tray
3. Bake for 1 hour till your mixture is caramelized.
4. Sauté the ginger and curry paste in a pan of the remaining oil.
5. Cook for 4 minutes.
6. Throw in the content of the baking tray.
7. Add in the stock.
8. Cook for 10 minutes.
9. Set aside to cool.
10. Blend the mixture in a fast food processor.
11. Pour the mixture into a pan.
12. Add the coconut milk.
13. Cook-stir for 4 minutes.
14. Throw in the lemon juice and herbs.
15. Serve

Barley Cream Soup

A simple but creamy serving of deliciousness!
 Preparation Time: 10 Minutes
 Cooking time: 30 Minutes
 Yield: 2

Ingredient List:

- 3 handfuls chopped pearl barley (blanched and drained)
- 100ml cream (thick)
- 15g melted butter
- 100ml milk
- 1 tablespoon pepper
- 1 tablespoon salt
- 1 liter chicken stock

Preparation:
1. Put the stock and barley in a pot.
2. Allow simmering for 25 minutes.
3. When barley is thickened, blend in a food processor.
4. Return to the pot. Then, add the butter, pepper, salt, cream, and milk.
5. Cook-stir for 4 minutes.
6. Serve and garnish with parsley.

Jalapeño syrup

You have heard of syrups, but we bet you haven't heard of this one!!
Preparation Time: 02 Minutes
Cooking time: 07 Minutes
Yield: 1

Ingredient List:

- 1 sliced jalapeño pepper
- 8 tablespoons water
- 1 cup demerara sugar

Preparation:
1. Boil the sugar in a pan of water.
2. Stir till the sugar is melted.
3. Throw in the jalapeño.
4. Cook for 4 minutes.
5. Set aside to cool and steep, and strain into a container.
6. Serve or store.

French Cider and Potato Soup

A quick trip to France won't hurt anyone, right?

Preparation Time: 10 Minutes
Cooking time: 15 Minutes
Yield: 2
Ingredient List:

- 1 sliced onion
- 20g melted butter
- 1 sliced potato

- 200ml chicken broth
- 60g cider
- 1 sliced jalapeño
- 1 sliced chili pepper
- 2 handfuls sliced apple (cut into matchsticks)
- 1 minced garlic clove
- 30ml crème fraîche
- 1 thyme sprig
- 30ml double cream

Preparation:
1. Sauté the garlic and onion in a pan of melted butter.
2. Cook for 3 minutes.
3. Add the thyme, potato, jalapeño, chili, and cider.
4. Cook for 6 minutes.
Toss in the cream, stock, and crème fraiche.
5. Cook for 7 minutes.
6. Discard thyme.
7. Blitz this mixture until it is creamy and smooth.
8. Serve and garnish with apple matchsticks.

Cauliflower Soup

This spicy soup is a perfect combo of creaminess and deliciousness!
Preparation Time: 03 Minutes
Cooking time: 10 Minutes
Yield: 2

Ingredient List:

- 2 tablespoons lemon juice
- 300g chopped cauliflower (divided)
- 1 teaspoon curry powder
- 2 tablespoons black pepper
- 1 tablespoon canola oil
- 60g Greek yogurt
- 1 cup chicken broth
- 1 minced garlic clove
- 1 chopped onion

Preparation:
1. Pour the oil in a pan.
2. Toss in a large part of the cauliflower.
3. Cook-stir for 6 minutes.
4. Add in the garlic and onion.
5. Cook for 2 minutes.
6. Throw in the curry and pepper.
7. Add in the broth.
8. Cook for 7 minutes.
9. Transfer the mixture and yogurt into your blender.
10. Blend well.
11. Serve and garnish with the remaining cauliflower and lemon juice.
12. Enjoy.

Spicy Green Juice

Dear green lovers, a little spice to spice your morning!!!
Preparation Time: 04 Minutes
Cooking time: Nil
Yield: 1

Ingredient List:

- 1 celery stalk
- 1 cucumber
- 1 seeded jalapeño
- 2 curly kale leaves
- 2 tablespoons hot sauce
- 1 pinch salt
- 2 tablespoons lemon juice
- 1 minced ginger piece
- 2 handfuls coriander

Preparation:
1. Fill your juicer with celery, jalapeño, kale, cucumber, coriander, and ginger.
2. Juice the mixture.
3. Strain into a glass.
4. Stir in the sauce, salt, and lemon juice.
5. Enjoy.

Lemon Delicious Pudding

This delicacy is an irony, like how can sour lemon be found in a delicious pudding? You are about to find out!!

Preparation Time: 08 Minutes
Cooking time: 20 Minutes
Yield: 3
Ingredient List:

- 6 tablespoons sifted flour
- 2 eggs (yolk)
- 80g melted butter
- 1 cup milk

- 2 tablespoons lemon juice
- 10 tablespoons caster sugar
- 2 tablespoons powder chili
- 1 tablespoon lemon rind (grated)
- 6 tablespoons Icing sugar mixture

Preparation:
1. Preheat the oven to 364 degrees F.
2. Drop the first 8 ingredients in a mixer.
3. Mix well.
4. Transfer to a baking pan.
5. Bake till it is well baked.
6. Serve and garnish with icing sugar mix.
7. Enjoy.

Butterscotch pudding

Absolutely spicily delicious!!!
   Preparation Time: 04 Minutes
   Cooking time: 10 Minutes
   Yield: 2

Ingredient List:

- 1 dash salt
- 4 tablespoons brown sugar
- 1 tablespoon cornstarch
- 8 tablespoons milk
- 1 teaspoon butter
- 1 teaspoon vanilla extract
- 8 tablespoons half and half
- 1 teaspoon butter
- 2 tablespoons cayenne pepper
- 1 pinch ground cinnamon

Preparation:
1. Mix the salt, sugar, and cornstarch in a pan.
2. Whisk well for 3 minutes.
3. Add the half and half.
4. Add milk.
5. Cook-stir for 6 minutes.
6. When the mixture starts to get thickened, turn off the heat.
7. Stir in cayenne pepper, cinnamon, butter, and vanilla.
8. Serve when chilled.

Jalapeño Margaritas

This margarita recipe will blow your palate away... not figuratively!!!
Preparation Time: 03 Minutes
Cooking time: Nil
Yield: 1

Ingredient List:

- 2 tablespoons silver tequila
- 2 lemon wedges
- 1 pinch salt
- 1 tablespoon agave nectar
- 1 tablespoon orange juice
- 2 tablespoons lemon juice
- 3 jalapeño pepper slices

Preparation:
1. Coat the rim of a glass with salt first.
2. Follow by a swipe of a lemon wedge around the rim.
3. Set glass aside in a refrigerator.
4. Put the jalapeño, juices, nectar, and tequila in a shaker.
5. Shake well.
6. Strain into your chilled glass.
7. Garnish with 2 jalapeño slices.
8. Enjoy.

Winter Warmer Soup

The name says it all!!
Preparation Time: 10 Minutes
Cooking time: 15 Minutes
Yield: 2

Ingredient List:

- 1 chopped celery
- 1 bay leaf
- 2 minced garlic cloves
- 1 minced ginger piece
- 2 tablespoons oil (divided)
- 1 tablespoon lemon juice
- 2 tablespoons chili powder
- 1 tablespoon turmeric powder
- 1 tablespoon cumin powder
- 2 cups broth
- 1 handful chopped coriander
- 1 tablespoon pepper
- 1 tablespoon salt
- 2 tablespoons chili garlic sauce
- 2 handfuls chopped mushrooms
- 2 boy chok slices

Preparation:
1. Sauté the boy chok, onions, and mushrooms in a pan of oil.
2. Cook for 3 minutes. Transfer to a plate. Set aside.
3. Sauté the bay leaf, celery, ginger, and garlic in a pan of oil.
4. Cook-stir for 6 minutes.
5. Add the cumin, pepper, chili powder, turmeric, and salt.
6. Cook for 2 minutes.
7. Add the broth and lemon juice and cook for 10 minutes.
8. Serve and garnish with the roasted mixture, chili garlic sauce, and coriander.
9. Enjoy.

Leek and Potato Soup

This combo sounds regular but tastes extraordinary!!
    Preparation Time: 10 Minutes
    Cooking time: 15 Minutes
    Yield: 3

Ingredient List:

- 1 pound peeled potatoes (chopped)
- 1 pinch salt
- 2 chopper chili peppers
- 1 minced garlic clove
- 1 bay leaf
- 3 cups chicken broth
- 2 large-sized leeks (chopped)
- 2 minced ginger pieces
- 2 sprigs thyme
- 1 tablespoon oil
- 8 tablespoons heavy cream
- 1 pinch black pepper
- 1 handful chopped chives

Preparation:
1. Sauté the ginger, garlic, and leek in a pan of oil.
2. Cook for 3 minutes.
3. Throw in the salt, potatoes, bay leaf, chilies, thyme, pepper, and broth.
4. Cook for 12 minutes.
5. Discard the bay leaf and thyme.
6. Puree the mixture.
7. Garnish with cream and chives.
8. Serve.

Thai Coconut Fish Stew

This recipe is another reason why we love Thailand!!

Preparation Time: 10 Minutes
Cooking time: 07 Minutes
Yield: 2
Ingredient List:

- 300ml coconut milk
- 300g white fish fillets (diced)
- 1 handful chopped cilantro leaves
- 2 tablespoons lemon juice
- 1 tablespoon brown sugar
- 150ml chicken broth
- 1 tablespoon canola oil
- 35ml fish sauce
- 1 cup spice paste
- 1 handful chopped choy sum

Preparation:
1. Sauté the spice paste in a wok of oil.
2. Cook for 3 minutes.
3. Add the broth, coconut milk, sauce, and sugar.
4. Cook for 4 minutes.
5. Add the choy sum and fillets.
6. Cook for 2 minutes before throwing in the lemon juice.
7. Serve. Garnish with cilantro.

Spicy Tequila Sunrise

Starting your winter morning with a glass of this cocktail is pure bliss!!
Preparation Time: 03 Minutes
Cooking time: Nil
Yield: 1

Ingredient List:

- 1 handful ice cubes
- 1 tablespoon agave syrup
- 3 jalapeño slices
- 1 oz lemon juice
- 1 oz silver tequila
- 3 oz orange juice
- 1 oz pomegranate juice
- 1 orange slice

Preparation:

1. Fill a shaker with syrup, lemon juice, orange juice, jalapeño, tequila, pomegranate juice, and ice cubes.
2. Shake well.
3. Strain into a glass. Garnish with jalapeño and orange slices.
4. Enjoy.

Conclusion

Beyond warm and thick winter wear, spicy meals and drinks are also good combatants of winter chills. Hence, here are 30 spicy foods and drinks that you can't do without this winter!!

Don't miss out!

Visit the website below and you can sign up to receive emails whenever Ida Smith publishes a new book. There's no charge and no obligation.

https://books2read.com/r/B-A-LRXL-AMUKB

BOOKS2READ

Connecting independent readers to independent writers.